MEXICO
BEAUTIFUL LAND
DIVERSE PEOPLE

THE FOOD OF MEXICO

JAN MCDANIEL

A Mexican woman buys tortillas from a vendor in Mexico City. Mexicans consume an estimated 30,000 tons of tortillas a day, sixty-five percent of which are hand made using traditional methods.

MEXICO
BEAUTIFUL LAND
DIVERSE PEOPLE

THE FOOD OF MEXICO

JAN MCDANIEL

Mason Crest Publishers
Philadelphia

Mason Crest Publishers
370 Reed Road
Broomall PA 19008
www.masoncrest.com

First printing

1 3 5 7 9 8 6 4 2

Library of Congress Cataloging-in-Publication Data on file at the Library of Congress

McDaniel, Jan.
  The food of Mexico / Jan McDaniel.
      p. cm. — (Mexico : beautiful land, diverse people)
  Includes bibliographical references.
  ISBN 978-1-4222-0655-3 (hardcover) — ISBN 978-1-4222-0722-2 (pbk.)
  1. Cookery, Mexican—History—Juvenile literature. 2. Food
habits—Mexico—History—Juvenile literature. I. Title.
  TX716.M4M3934 2008
  641.5972—dc22
                                    2008031853

TABLE OF CONTENTS

MEXICO
BEAUTIFUL LAND
DIVERSE PEOPLE

INTRODUCTION

Mexico is a country in the midst of great change. And what happens in Mexico reverberates in the United States, its neighbor to the north.

For outsiders, the most obvious of Mexico's recent changes has occurred in the political realm. From 1929 until the end of the 20th century, the country was ruled by a single political party: the Partido Revolucionario Institucional, or PRI (in English, the Institutional Revolutionary Party). Over the years, PRI governments became notorious for corruption, and the Mexican economy languished. In 2000, however, the PRI's stranglehold on national politics was broken with the election of Vicente Fox as Mexico's president. Fox, of the Partido de Acción Nacional (National Action Party), or PAN, promised political reform and economic development but had a mixed record as president. However, another PAN candidate, Felipe Calderón, succeeded Fox in 2006 after a hotly contested and highly controversial election. That election saw Calderón win by the slimmest of margins over a candidate from the Partido de la Revolución Democrática (Party of the Democratic Revolution). The days of one-party rule in Mexico, it seems, are gone for good.

Mexico's economy, like its politics, has seen significant changes in recent years. A 1994 free-trade agreement with the United States and Canada, along with the increasing transfer of industries from government control to private ownership under President Fox and President Calderón, has helped spur economic growth in Mexico. When all the world's countries are compared,

Mexico now falls into the upper-middle range in per-capita income. This means that, on average, Mexicans enjoy a higher standard of living than people in the majority of the world's countries. Yet averages can be misleading. In Mexico there is an enormous gap between haves and have-nots. According to some estimates, 40 percent of the country's more than 100 million people live in poverty. In some areas of Mexico, particularly in rural villages, jobs are almost nonexistent. This has driven millions of Mexicans to immigrate to the United States (with or without proper documentation) in search of a better life.

By 2006 more than 11 million people born in Mexico were living in the United States (including more than 6 million illegal immigrants), according to estimates based on data from the Pew Hispanic Center and the U.S. Census Bureau. Meanwhile, nearly one of every 10 people living in the United States was of Mexican ancestry. Clearly, Mexico and Mexicans have had—and will continue to have—a major influence on American society.

It is especially unfortunate, then, that many American students know little about their country's neighbor to the south. The books in the MEXICO: BEAUTIFUL LAND, DIVERSE PEOPLE series are designed to help correct that.

As readers will discover, Mexico boasts a rich, vibrant culture that is a blend of indigenous and European—especially Spanish—influences. More than 3,000 years ago, the Olmec people created a complex society and built imposing monuments that survive to this day in the Mexican states of Tabasco and Veracruz. In the fifth century A.D., when the Roman Empire collapsed and Europe entered its so-called Dark Age, the Mayan civilization was already flourishing in the jungles of the Yucatán Peninsula—and it would enjoy another four centuries of tremendous cultural achievements. By the time the Spanish conqueror Hernán Cortés landed at Veracruz in 1519, another great indigenous civilization, the Aztecs, had emerged to dominate much of Mexico.

With a force of about 500 soldiers, plus a few horses and cannons, Cortés marched inland toward the Aztec capital, Tenochtitlán. Built in the middle of a lake in what is now Mexico City, Tenochtitlán was an engineering marvel and one of the largest cities anywhere in the world at the time. With allies from among the indigenous peoples who resented being ruled by the Aztecs—and aided by a smallpox epidemic—Cortés and the Spaniards managed to conquer the Aztec Empire in 1521 after a brutal fight that devastated Tenochtitlán.

It was in that destruction that modern Mexico was born. Spaniards married indigenous people, creating mestizo offspring—as well as a distinctive Mexican culture that was neither Spanish nor indigenous but combined elements of both.

Spain ruled Mexico for three centuries. After an unsuccessful revolution in 1810, Mexico finally won its independence in 1821.

But the newly born country continued to face many difficulties. Among them were bad rulers, beginning with a military officer named Agustín Iturbide, who had himself crowned emperor only a year after Mexico threw off the yoke of Spain. In 1848 Mexico lost a war with the United States—and was forced to give up almost half of its territory as a result. During the 1860s French forces invaded Mexico and installed a puppet emperor. While Mexico regained its independence in 1867 under national hero Benito Juárez, the long dictatorship of Porfirio Díaz would soon follow.

Díaz was overthrown in a revolution that began in 1910, but Mexico would be racked by fighting until the Partido Revolucionario Institucional took over in 1929. The PRI brought stability and economic progress, but its rule became increasingly corrupt.

Today, with the PRI's long monopoly on power swept away, Mexico stands on the brink of a new era. Difficult problems such as entrenched inequalities and grinding poverty remain. But progress toward a more open political system may lead to economic and social progress as well. Mexico—a land with a rich and ancient heritage—may emerge as one of the 21st century's most inspiring success stories.

Tacos are one of Mexico's most recognized dishes. The American version of the taco, shown here, is different from the type most Mexicans eat, however. For instance, Mexicans are unlikely to request a hard-shelled taco.

1

AZTEC TREASURES

t's been said Mexican cooks can turn the most meager ingredients into pure gold. Mexico boasts one of the oldest forms of original cooking, dating back to the Aztec civilization. Since those ancient times, Mexicans' skill and imagination have transformed simple foods into culinary treasures. Through hard work and precision, corn becomes **tortillas** and **tamales**. Beans simmer into hardy stews. Chilies add unique flavors to rich sauces.

At home and in restaurants, Americans today enjoy meals based on genuine Mexican **cuisine**. But these Americanized versions of Mexican foods resemble the originals only slightly. Restaurant owners who offer food too authentic to satisfy American tastes find staying in business difficult.

As Mexican food manufacturer Francisco "Frank" Morales explains,

EASY GUACAMOLE

2 large avocados, peeled and pits removed
2 teaspoons lemon juice
$1/3$ cup salsa

1. *In medium bowl, mash avocados with a fork.*
2. *Add lemon juice and salsa; stir until blended.*
3. *Refrigerate until serving. Makes approximately $1^1/2$ cups.*

Americans like Mexican dishes made with ground beef, while true Mexican cooks use center cuts of beef, pork, mutton, goat, chicken, and turkey. Also, most Americans prefer sweet tomato-based sauces to traditional bitter chili sauces. The menu of a Mexican-style restaurant in the United States might center on tacos, **enchiladas**, and **quesadillas**. In Mexico, these items, known as *antojitos*, are eaten as snacks or appetizers.

The Mexican food we know started with the Aztecs. A highly sophisticated people, the Aztecs were growing corn and preparing tamales and tortillas long before Spanish explorers arrived in 1519. Eventually, as the Spanish conquered and colonized Mexico, European cooks brought new ingredients, recipes, and food preparation methods. Traditional Indian foods took new twists.

The tortilla is an excellent example of these changes. Indians ate the thin corn pancakes alone or used them as the basis for more complex dishes. After the Spanish imported wheat, tortillas made with flour instead of ground corn became one of the first innovations. Flour tortillas remain popular throughout modern Mexico, especially in the north.

Throughout Mexico's 300 years as a Spanish colony, Europeans, Americans, Asians, and other ethnic groups influenced the native Mexican cuisine. This gradual blending of heritages is known as *mestizaje*. Most native people enjoyed the same foods their ancestors had eaten, but European cooking reigned as the preference of the upper classes. Not until the 1940s, well after winning independence, did Mexicans begin reviving old recipes and claiming their own national cuisine.

The writings of Spanish explorer Hernán Cortés and the men who

A Mexican woman cooks tortillas in her home. The corn tortillas bake on a sheet over an open flame, while a pot of seasoned rice or meat is prepared as a filling.

traveled with him reveal much about how the Aztecs lived. Tales of Aztec wealth first drew Cortés to Tenochtitlán, the Aztecs' capital city. Cortés landed along Mexico's Yucatán coast in March 1519 and conquered the town of Tabasco. Natives there described the riches of the Aztec empire. Excited by their stories, Cortés continued his quest.

The Aztec empire was highly advanced in many ways. The Aztecs had built on knowledge from earlier native cultures to become skilled in art, astronomy, mathematics, writing, calendars, music, sculpture, metalwork, textiles and weaving, architecture, and farming. Aztec farmers irrigated their fields with canal systems. In orchards they grew avocados, coconuts, papayas, and pineapples. They raised green tomatoes, chilies, sweet potatoes, squash, peanuts, beans, and herbs, but kept few domestic animals.

The peanut was known to the Aztecs as *tlalcachuatl*, "earth peanut." Today's Spanish word for peanut—*cacahuate*—comes from this ancient Aztec word.

While the nobles enjoyed a lavish lifestyle, most natives lived simply. They wore cotton clothing and built wood or stone houses. Unlike the rulers who ate meat or fish, common people survived on a vegetarian diet, mainly corn. They ate corn tortillas and flavored cornmeal porridge called *atole*; beans seasoned with chilies, bananas, and wild papaya; and guacamole made from avocados. They drank *pulque*, an alcoholic beverage made from the partially fermented sap

The ancient Mexicans offered sacrifices to certain gods to ensure a bountiful harvest. This statue is a representation of Xilonen, a seasonal goddess.

of the maguey cactus plant.

Meanwhile, Aztec rulers feasted on elaborate banquets including stewed meats in chili sauce or *molé*, fried bananas, boiled nopal cactus, and tamales. Nobles achieved fame and status by serving tortillas, stew, and hot or cold chocolate drinks to their guests. Their cooks shaped tortillas like butterflies or leaves. Food for feasts stayed warm in *chafing dishes*. The Aztecs observed certain table manners, holding tortillas properly, using cotton napkins, and not stuffing their mouths or slurping. Music and dancing frequently ended a banquet. Occasionally, royal feasts served as charity to feed the poor.

Because the Aztecs depended on nature for survival, it is not surprising they worshipped the sun. Food, especially corn, which originated in Mexico, was considered a gift from the gods. According to Mayan and Aztec myths, the gods had molded humans from corn dough. To ensure a good harvest, ancient people did whatever they believed necessary to keep their gods happy, strong, and generous so their crops would grow.

At a festival held during the dry season, the Aztecs asked Chicomecóatl (also called Xilonen), the goddess of sustenance, to bless seed corn. Depicted as a young woman in red wearing a tiara, corn necklace, and holding ears of corn, she was associated with abundance and fertility. To honor the goddess, maidens danced on flower petals in the fields. The god Centéotl reigned over the harvest. Some Aztec religious

From the maguey cactus, also called Mexican aloe, Aztecs made beverages, sweeteners, fabric, paper, needles and pins, and shingles for their houses.

Tamales are a popular food for meals and snacks in Mexico. They consist of cornhusks filled with cornmeal dough and a mixture of fried meat and peppers.

In this tiled sculpture, Quetzalcoatl is depicted emerging from the jaws of the earth. A major creator god of the Aztecs and Toltecs, he is said to have introduced agriculture to Mexico.

offerings involved human sacrifices. Sometimes they killed prisoners of war or slaves as sacrifices, and for such cruelty other tribes feared and hated them.

Founded in 1325, the Aztec capital, Tenochtitlán, occupied an island in Lake Texcoco. Linked to the mainland by causeways and protected by dams, Tenochtitlán was a city of large houses, palaces, and pyramids. Every day, the market brought in some 60,000 vendors and shoppers. They bartered for pottery, fabrics, arrows, tools, and food in exchange for gold, stamped tin, or cocoa beans.

Aztec Emperor Montezuma II, the ninth Aztec king, ruled from 1502 to 1520. Known as a harsh tyrant, when he learned of the Spaniards' landing, he contemplated how to act toward them. Montezuma believed Cortés was connected to Quetzalcoatl, a light-skinned, bearded Aztec god predicted to return in the year of the Spaniards' arrival. Dressed in jewels, feathers, and gold, Montezuma and about 200 nobles marching in two columns met Cortés and his men as they reached the city's entrance. The blending of Indian and European heritage began here, as two cultures with contrasting customs, religion, and beliefs came together for the first time. A Spanish-speaking Indian woman named La Malinche—called Doña Marina by the Spaniards—acted as interpreter.

In a peaceful gesture, the two leaders exchanged necklaces. Cortés assured Montezuma he came as an **ambassador**. The emperor promised Cortés anything he asked. Montezuma welcomed the Spanish as honored guests. They shared a lavish banquet of turkey stew and white tortillas, and Montezuma invited Cortés to stay in the palace. In return, Cortés took Montezuma hostage.

The Aztecs drove the Spanish from Tenochititlán in a battle known as *la noche triste*, the sorrowful night. But the Spanish possessed better weapons and battle strategy. Montezuma's savagery toward conquered tribes prompted other Indians, especially the Tlascalans, to fight with the Spanish. The **conquistadors** also brought **smallpox**, and many Aztecs died from the previously unknown disease. By 1521, the Spanish had

Montezuma enjoyed frozen confections flavored with fruit or chocolate. He was said to have sent runners up a mountain to bring ice for his treats.

defeated the Aztecs. Cortés occupied and destroyed Tenochititlán. He later founded Mexico City on the site.

Mexico remained a Spanish colony until 1821. The Spanish had come to Mexico not only for wealth, but to spread the Roman Catholic religion. As friars, monks, priests, and nuns brought Christianity, European customs and cookery accompanied them. But as Mexico's original native cuisine, Aztec cooking formed the foundation for all later Mexican cooking. Names of many modern Mexican dishes stem from words in the Aztec language, Nahuatl.

Because life in ancient Mexico depended on preparing food in addition to growing it, the native Mexicans had developed clever ways to process food. They invented equipment for mashing and grilling and found ways to season food and make it taste better. Without the convenience of electric appliances, cooking was very hard work.

Using the *metate*, a flat, slanted grinding stone, they ground chilies, tomatoes, cornmeal, or pumpkinseeds into thick sauces they called *molli*. Seasoned beans simmered slowly in clay pots, *cazuelas*, set over hot coals. Mashing chilies and tart fruits called *tomatillos* with avocado flavored their guacamole. Wrapping food in leaves gave it a special flavor while roasting. Tamales were steamed in cornhusks. Other foods were roasted in banana leaves or maguey leaves.

The history of Mexican food comes to us

Before humans learned to cultivate crops, they survived by hunting and gathering wild plants. Ancient Mexicans began farming at least 8,000 years ago. After analyzing seeds discovered in a Mexican cave, scientists determined early varieties of pumpkins and summer squash were grown as crops.

in many ways. We know what the Aztecs ate from descriptions written by Cortés and his companions, who were astonished by all they saw. We also know about the Aztecs' cuisine because it is still practiced. Through the centuries, residents of small villages have continued making tortillas and tamales in the old way. Chefs and cookbook authors have visited Mexican communities to research recipes passed down through generations. In addition, modern researchers can identify ingredients used in ancient foods by studying residue on pottery fragments.

Before his captivity, Montezuma's diet reflected his power and prestige as emperor. He feasted daily on hundreds of dishes prepared by his servants. In his banquet hall, the Spanish sampled foods made from ingredients they had never tasted before. Here and in the market, the newcomers saw tortillas, tamales, wild turkey, quail, duck, frogs, newts, lobsters, corn, squash, beans, avocado, tomatoes, squash, cactus, shrimp, herring, partridge, and other Aztec delights.

Drinking chocolate, one of Montezuma's favorite treats, represented the ultimate indulgence, reserved only for nobles. The Aztecs prized cacao beans so much they used them as money. To make a hot or cold beverage, they ground the beans, known to them as *xoxoc-atl*, into powder. They added water, honey, and flavorings such as vanilla or pepper. Unlike the hot chocolate we enjoy on a wintry day, this drink contained no sugar and no milk. The Spanish quickly grew fond of chocolate, but after it was imported to Europe, a controversy arose over whether it was too decadent and might corrupt those who drank it. Hundreds of years later, the English began preparing cocoa with milk.

Tortillas are a *staple* of the Mexican diet, and there is a movement to make them more nutritious. Corn flour used to make the tortillas is now enriched with soy, vitamins, and minerals in an effort to improve the health of impoverished children.

2

THE INCREDIBLE TORTILLA

The invention of the tortilla constitutes one of the ancient world's most amazing cooking feats. From plain corn, the Aztecs created a versatile flat bread with lasting appeal. The Spanish created the word tortillas from their word *torta*, meaning round cake. Tortillas packed easily for a journey or festival. Folded, they wrapped other foods or made an edible scoop for stew or beans. Flat, they formed a makeshift platter. Cooked crisp into a tostada, they stayed fresh for a long time. Centuries later, on America's western *frontier*, tortillas became favored camp chow after Mexican vaqueros introduced them to the other cowboys.

Although tortillas were introduced throughout the United States only within the past 50 years, today they enjoy global popularity. Frito-Lay first marketed tortilla chips in 1966. Ready-made tortillas for home cooking didn't become generally available in American stores until 1990. They caught on so fast that by 1996

According to legend, a Mayan peasant invented the tortilla for his king.

24

Americans were eating more than 64 billion a year. Modern American shoppers buy more tortillas than any other ethnic and specialty breads, including muffins, bagels, and croissants. Varieties flavored with spinach, tomato, or garlic are gaining popularity. In recent decades, tortillas have even traveled to outer space, feeding NASA crewmembers.

Making corn tortillas is no simple task. The process requires time, patience, physical strength, and skill. First, the corn must soak overnight in water containing **lime**. This process, called *nixtamalización*, softens the corn kernels so the outer shells can be removed. It also slightly changes the corn's flavor. The Aztecs used lime from oyster shells and other seashells and from limestone. What they didn't know was that soaking the corn in lime also released amino acids and made the corn more nutritious. Once softened, the corn is ground into dough called *masa* to make tortillas, tamales, and other foods.

Rolling out tortillas is a delicate process that requires a great deal of practice and skill. It is important that the tortillas be neither too thick nor too thin, or they will not cook as well.

TORTILLAS DE HARINA (FLOUR TORTILLAS)

2 cups flour
1 teaspoon salt
$1/3$ cup vegetable shortening
$1/2$ cup warm water

1. *Mix together flour and salt in a bowl.*
2. *Cut in the shortening, then add water to make a stiff dough.*
3. *Knead on a lightly floured board.*
4. *Form dough into 8 small balls.*
5. *Let dough stand 15 minutes.*
6. *With a heavy wooden rolling pin, roll balls to paper-thin thickness and brown in a lightly greased skillet. Turn with spatula.*
7. *Eat or cool, then store in a sealed plastic bag.*

A man buys tortillas from a local vendor in Mexico City. The Mexican government sets the market price for tortillas, ensuring that poor families will be able to afford this staple of the Mexican diet. The government is currently considering the implications of ending this practice, however.

was patented in 1899, and Mexico's first tortilla factory opened in 1902. Even *tortillerías*, Mexican stores specializing in tortillas, ultimately switched from selling handmade tortillas to mass-produced ones.

Tortillas are manufactured through a process beginning with ground masa poured into a bin, then mixed into dough. Stamped tortillas pop out through a press at the bottom. They travel along a conveyor belt over a hot flame in an oven, flip over to cook on the other side, then fall into a basket.

In Mexico, more people are now buying manufactured tortillas in supermarkets. Ready-made tortillas provide convenience, but they may not taste the same as homemade. Shoppers who prefer fresh handmade tortillas can purchase them from vendors.

Since January 2001, Mexican tortillas must be made from only white corn. The government passed this measure to prevent humans from eating genetically altered yellow corn until tests determine whether it is safe for humans and the environment. Researchers had changed yellow corn by modifying seeds to make the plants resist insects and tolerate certain weed killers. After eating foods containing altered corn, about 15 people reported allergic reactions, including stomach problems and sneezing. Ecological organizations such as

Inventor Luis Romero Soto was born in San Juan del Río in 1876. As a boy, he fashioned an alarm clock from a string, candle, and kitchen utensils to wake himself up for school. As a teenager, he invented an automatic postage machine. Although he made his living designing ironwork for mansions, he invented and patented a tortilla machine. Afterward, he opened the first tortilla factory and began mass marketing manufactured tortillas.

Otomí Indians carry bags of enriched corn flour for making healthier tortillas. In initial studies, the nutritional additives appear to be improving the health of impoverished Mexican families.

Tortillas can be baked or fried until crispy chips and served with salsa, a snack that Americans have adopted from Mexico. Although Americans are most familiar with salsa made from tomatoes, onions, and peppers, there are other varieties as well, including fruit salsa made with mango or pineapple.

Greenpeace protested the sale of cereal and tortillas made with genetically altered corn. In the autumn of 2000, these products were removed from stores until proven safe. There are no known genetically altered strains of white corn.

Flour tortillas are somewhat easier to make than corn tortillas, because the dough is rolled into disks instead of patted by hand. Keeping them small makes the dough easier to handle. Perfect tortillas require practice. Developing the knack takes a few tries.

The world's largest tortilla measured 14$^1/_2$ feet across. The townspeople of Oaxaca constructed it as a challenge in May 2000. Later, they filled it with 70 pounds of cheese and beef, 54 pounds of beans, and 5 gallons of salsa to form the world's largest taco.

3

SPANISH INFLUENCES

Monks and nuns arriving in New Spain to spread Christianity brought with them European cooking techniques. The nuns were smart, resourceful, and educated in domestic skills—like embroidery, needlepoint, and cooking. Their convent kitchen innovations mixed Spanish and Indian cuisine to create new fare.

Back in early colonial days, religious orders made the first impact on native cookery, although their real mission was to convert Indians. By the end of Spanish rule, millions of natives had accepted the Catholic religion.

In addition to their religious duties, nuns prepared confections to earn income for their orders or as gifts for influential officials. They did this so expertly, many convents became well known for their candies, custards, puddings, and other sweets. The Santa Rosa Convent in Puebla

A candy store employee organizes a window display of marzipan. The confection is made from crushed almonds or almond paste, sugar, and egg whites, then formed into decorative, and often colorful, shapes.

grew famous for *camotes*, long strips of candied sweet potatoes. In Mexico City, the Convent of San Francisco specialized in *aleluyas*, almond and cinnamon candies given as Easter presents. Other convents earned reputations for chocolates, **marzipan**, or jam-filled crescents called *fruta de horno*. Nuns mixed Old World and New World ingredients and skills to create these goodies.

Frequently in Mexico today, candy is served as dessert, but the custom of eating dessert after a meal comes from Europe. When the sisters lacked ingredients for a favorite recipe they brought with them, they substituted native foods. The Spanish brought milk, eggs, sugar, and almonds, and they made use of Mexican chocolate, coconut, and other fruits and nuts. The Aztecs sweetened dishes with honey or cactus juice. The Spanish brought and planted sugar, which thrived

32

MOLLETES DE CALABAZA (PUMPKIN MUFFINS)

1 cup canned pumpkin
$^1/_2$ cup milk
1 egg, well-beaten
$^1/_2$ cup sugar
2 tablespoons melted margarine
1 teaspoon nutmeg
1 teaspoon cinnamon
$1^1/_2$ cups flour
1 teaspoon salt
3 teaspoons baking powder

1. *Preheat the oven to 400 degrees Fahrenheit.*
2. *Mix the pumpkin and milk, then add the egg, sugar, melted margarine, and spices.*
3. *In a separate mixing bowl, stir the flour, salt, and baking powder together.*
4. *Stir the dry ingredients into the pumpkin mixture.*
5. *Pour into greased muffin tins, filling them about half full, and bake 25 minutes.*

Many Mexicans buy their food from street markets rather than from grocery stores. The blackberries and chilies in this display are probably fresher and more affordable than prepackaged food.

An Indian woman grills fresh corn on the cob at a market stall in Mexico. Corn is probably the most important crop in the traditional Mexican diet, as it can be used in almost any dish. Scientists believe corn evolved from wild grains that cross-pollinated by chance some 10,000 years ago.

in the tropical regions.

In their gardens, the sisters planted seeds and cuttings of Old World plants, carrots, onions, peas, cabbage, to see what would grow in the Mexican climate. Not all plants could survive. They found concocting a heavy paste or jam known as *ate* preserved fruit in the tropical climate. Sometimes, the nuns requested help from native women familiar with the local foods.

The most famous legend in all Mexican cooking history centers on an original stew created by a Spanish nun. Her *molé poblano de guajolote*, or turkey in molé sauce, became Mexico's national dish. Festive fare, *molé poblano* comes in many variations and is served at all celebrations.

As the story goes, one day in the 1680s, Sor Andrea de la Asunción of the Santa Rosa Convent in Puebla de los Angeles hoped to prepare an unforgettable meal to impress a visiting dignitary, either an archbishop or a viceroy. As she began cooking, she cut up and boiled a turkey

MEXICAN WEDDING CAKES

$1/2$ pound butter
$1/2$ cup sugar
1 teaspoon vanilla
green food coloring
2 cups sifted all-purpose flour
1 cup pecans, finely chopped
confectioners' sugar

1. *Cream the butter. Add the sugar and vanilla; cream until light and fluffy.*
2. *Add a few drops of food coloring to tint a light green.*
3. *Add the flour and pecans; mix well.*
4. *Roll into one-inch balls and place an inch apart on an ungreased cookie sheet.*
5. *Bake in a 325-degree oven for 18 to 20 minutes, or until lightly browned.*
6. *Remove from the cookie sheet and roll in confectioners' sugar while warm. Makes about $4^1/2$ dozen balls.*

A Mexican nun wears a sombrero for a festival parade. Nuns and missionaries from Spain influenced the concept of sweets in Mexico when they introduced candies and desserts to the native taste.

with tomatoes. Employing Indian methods, she toasted red and black chilies, then ground them into paste on a *metate*. As the mixture simmered, she added cloves, cinnamon, peppercorns, coriander, sesame seeds, other seasonings, and ground tortillas. As a final inspiration, she added chocolate. She may have hoped the chocolate would tone down the spiciness or maybe she simply wanted to make her creation unique. One variation of the legend says that Sor Andrea accidentally spilled an entire tray of spices into the pot where the *molé* was cooking, creating the unique blend of flavors.

Accident or not, the important visitor approved. Spanish

Wild turkey got its name from 16th-century Europeans, who mistakenly believed the imported birds had come from Turkey rather than Mexico.

missionaries began serving *molé poblano* at religious celebrations, and the dish became a favorite throughout Mexico. The idea of chocolate chili sauce on turkey may sound unappetizing if you imagine a candy bar melted in stew. But what is actually used is a tiny piece of unsweetened Mexican chocolate.

Despite *molé poblano's* popularity, recipes for it weren't printed until the middle 1800s. Preparing *molé poblano* presents a major task. It requires at least eight hours, usually over several days, and from 20 to 30 ingredients, depending on the recipe. Chilies must be roasted, spices ground. At **fiesta** time, residents of some towns set up an assembly line to make molé.

The Spanish also changed the way native Mexicans ate by importing the first domestic animals to Mexico. The Spaniards brought cattle, pigs, chickens, sheep, goats, horses, donkeys, and mules. Conquistadors obtained land grants to create ranches where they raised their cattle. Eventually, the Indians acquired a taste for beef, pork, and chicken, and worked them into native recipes. For example, they began making tamales with pork fat.

The Spanish liked breads baked with wheat flour, the kind they had eaten at home. Because the Catholic Church considered wheat the only acceptable grain for Communion wafers, efforts to replace native grains with wheat flour became a religious matter. The

The Spanish brought and cultivated the radish during the colonial days. Today, radishes are often carved into roses to garnish Mexican dishes. In Oaxaca, an annual Christmas celebration, Night of the Radishes, features sculptures shaped from long red radishes, flowers, and dried cornhusks.

The view through the archway of the Santa Rosa convent, which became known for the nuns' delicious camotes. Their cooking skill and ingenuity produced unique recipes that are still enjoyed by Mexicans today.

Europeans also believed wheat provided more nutrition than corn. The natives loved corn, however, and at first the Spanish couldn't even give wheat bread away to beggars. Colonists planted wheat fields, though, and eventually, the Indians who tended them ate the bread they received as wages.

Early in Mexico's history, bakeries were held in low regard. Criminals were forced to work there as punishment. As a result of French influences after the Spanish occupation ended, however, wonderful bakeries flourish throughout Mexico today. Shoppers choose from an assortment of rolls, *crêpes*, pastries, breads, and sweet breads. Traditional wheat bread is baked in a brick oven with a wood fire and contains no preservatives.

The Spanish also brought to Mexico the process of sautéing or frying foods in fats. They exported native Mexican foods—pineapple, wild turkey, cocoa, sweet potatoes, squash, pumpkins and peanuts—to Europe.

Many convents shut down in the 19th and 20th centuries as the church lost its influence in Mexico. The church's increasing wealth and power had triggered reforms against church control, and the government implemented restrictions against the church. Under Mexico's 1857 constitution the church could no longer own property, and the convent in Puebla closed. Today, it is a national monument. Puebla remains Mexico's candy capital, famed for sweet shops offering marzipan molded into various shapes, candied figs, guava paste, and of course *camotes*.

The native Mexicans categorized hot peppers as ají and sweet peppers as chilies.

Bacalao is a popular dish made with cod, a type of fish that can be caught along the coast of Mexico.

FEASTS AND FIESTAS

4

Ever since baskets of tamales circulated at Aztec banquets, Mexican food has meant life, happiness, and celebration. The Mexican people find much cause for rejoicing. Mexico observes 15 national holidays and countless local festivals and fiestas. No family milestone—whether a christening, graduation, planting, wedding, First Communion, birthday, saint's day, or funeral—passes without a party and feasting. In addition, any workday that falls between two holidays, becomes a *puente*, a day of rest.

The word fiesta comes from the Latin *festa*, meaning joyous. A fiesta provides a break from everyday life and an occasion to honor family, friends, church, or country. Just as native Mexican cuisine blended with influences of other cultures, fiestas may reflect the coming together of ancient ritual, Spanish culture, and Christian religion. A solemn occasion may be marked by a colorful explosion of merriment—music, dancing, costumes. Always, good food abounds.

Roman Catholicism remains the predominant Mexican faith. Every city, town, and village holds a fiesta to honor its patron saint's day and give thanks for protection and blessings. Traditionally, a prosperous local businessman or farmer sponsors the fiesta. Supplying the meat or other food represents a privilege and a way to thank God for good fortune. Festivities take place in the neighborhood plaza, the heart of the community. Businesses close for anywhere from one day to a week while festivities are underway. Celebrations may involve masks, costumes, pageants, bullfights, a pilgrimage, a special religious service, games, horsemanship, fireworks, singing, dancing, or giant puppets. Food vendors set up booths nearby.

A unique Mexican holiday blending ancient ritual with religious elements is the Day of the Dead, *El Día de los Muertos*. Despite its grim-sounding name, this happy holiday actually embraces life by honoring ancestors. The festival lasts three days, October 31 through November 2, the same days as All Hallows Eve, All Saints Day, and All Souls Day.

Long ago, the Aztecs believed success in life required showing proper respect for the dead. To help souls journey to Mictlán, their land of the dead, they built shrines on which they placed images of the departed and offerings of fruit and flowers. Today, during the Day of the Dead, Mexicans heap gifts to deceased loved ones on homemade altars. They await the return of their ancestors' souls to earth for one day. Skulls, crossbones, and skeletons, symbols of life in ancient Mexico, appear as figures, costumes, masks, and candy.

Day of the Dead celebrations vary through different regions of Mexico. In some villages, families build altars for their offerings—*ofrendas*—in their homes. Local church bells ring to summon returning souls, and fireworks explode to welcome them. In other places, Mexican families travel to graveyards on October 31 and stay through the entire

Mexican cuisine is often colorful, due to the combinations of ripe vegetables, meat, and tortillas that are a part of almost every meal. Enchiladas, burritos, and tacos can have similar contents but are prepared differently.

Red beans, sold here from a sack in a market stall, round out a healthy Mexican meal. They can be eaten with rice, or included in the filling for tortillas.

holiday. There, they build altars and stack them with religious statues, poems, candles, and gifts of favorite foods and objects their loved one enjoyed in life. Bright bundles of flowers—yellow marigolds the Aztecs called *zempoalxóchitl,* known in Mexico as the flower of the dead; bright red *terciopelo,* or cockscomb; and baby's breath—also top these altars. Food offerings frequently include tamales, molé, fruit, hot chocolate, and a special holiday bread, *pan de muertos.*

"Bread for the dead" is one variety of Mexico's hundreds of *pan dulces* (sweet breads). Bakeries prepare it especially for the holiday. Round loaves are coated with licorice-flavored sugary syrup and decorated with crossbones. Some families order one loaf baked for each deceased relative. Sometimes homemade papier-mâché faces are tucked into the loaves.

Another Day of the Dead specialty, *calaveras,* are molded sugar figures decorated with colored icing. Children write their names on sugar skulls and place them on the altars. Artists in Toluca, Mexico, begin working as early as May each year to create skull-, animal-, flower-, or coffin-shaped sugar figures. Through a process called *alfeñique,* they shape a mixture of sugar, egg whites, and food coloring in clay molds. Once the figures dry and harden, they are painted with icing.

On November 1, after a light breakfast, families tend gravesites. They may share their evening meal of tamales and molé with departed loved ones by placing portions on the altars. Throughout that night they hold candlelight vigils, praying and burning

According to custom, *buñuelos* purchased at sidewalk stands in Oaxaca are served in pottery dishes. Once the pancakes are eaten, the dishes are smashed.

incense, while awaiting the returning souls. Food vendors set up stalls nearby. The spirits of the dead are believed to return and join the festivities on November 2. The celebration peaks with picnics, bands, balloons, songs, games, and fireworks.

As important as the Day of the Dead is to Mexican culture, Christmas is Mexico's most important holiday. The traditional Mexican Christmas celebration begins with Las Posadas on December 16 and lasts through the Epiphany on January 6. On December 16, Mexican families display elaborate nativity sets. Figures collected over many years may represent a tiny village with details like tiny cactus plants. The nativity may even include a figurine depicting a woman kneeling at a metate making tortillas. According to tradition, the baby Jesus figure is not placed in the manger until December 24.

December 16 also begins the first of nine symbolic processions combining religion and fun. These are called *Posadas* (meaning "refuges" or "shelters"). Local processions portray Mary and Joseph's journey from Nazareth to Bethlehem. Along the way, the participants sing hymns and knock on doors. At each stop, they are turned away until they reach their true destination. Here, a party is planned. Along with holiday foods, tamales, **buñuelos**, hot chocolate, and cakes, there may be fireworks. Blindfolded children swing sticks to break open a piñata. The decorated papier-mâché piñatas are filled with small sweets, cookies, peanuts, and fruit.

An agave plant thrives in the desert of Baja California Sur. Sap from the leaves of the agave can be distilled to make tequila.

The Day of the Dead festival honors the spirits of those who have passed away. On this day, Mexicans decorate the graves of their loved ones with "bread for the dead," a symbolic gesture to their well-being in the afterlife.

In Mexico, as most places, Christmas means making favorite dishes from old family recipes. Festive foods vary between regions and individual families. Entire families may pitch in to fry batches of buñuelos. These Christmas treats are sometimes exchanged as gifts.

Christmas Eve and Christmas Day mean a quiet celebration at home. Families share a Christmas Eve dinner, attend midnight mass, and exchange presents. The American customs of decorating a tree, exchanging gifts on Christmas, and roasting a turkey have only recently become popular. While wild turkey is native to Mexico, holiday turkey has usually been served as molé poblano.

Other traditional Christmas dishes include *bacalao*, an extravagant European creation of dried cod soaked, reconstituted, and baked with oil and spices in a slow oven; *revoltijo*, dried shrimp patties and vegetables cooked in molé; and *pierna*, leg of pork. Flavored with sugar, cinnamon, or mint and fruits such as oranges, strawberries, and lime, *Ponche de Navidad* (Christmas punch) is served warm or over ice. The colorful Christmas Eve salad, *Ensalada de Noche Buena*, contains beets, ***jícama***, oranges, and peanuts. While many Mexican dishes are garnished with vegetables, this ranks as probably the only authentic Mexican salad. Americans invented taco salad.

The custom of serving tamales at all Mexican celebrations dates back perhaps as far as A.D. 750. Making tamales requires so much time and work, they are usually prepared at home only for special celebrations. Families or neighbors line up to cook in assembly-line fashion. Normally, a mixture of corn dough, broth, chili sauce, and chopped meat or beans is wrapped in cornhusks, which are folded and steamed. Tamales differ according to tastes and regions. They may be wrapped in banana leaves instead of cornhusks or flavored with molé. Fillings might be made from beef, pork, shrimp, fish, pumpkin, pineapple, or even wild cherries. Sweet tamales with raisins, candied fruit, cinnamon, or pecans are preferred in some regions, especially at Christmastime. Some tamales contain no filling.

Since ancient times, the beverages *pulque* or *atole* were always served with tamales. Now considered old-fashioned, that custom has been abandoned for modern drinks such as soda or coffee.

The Christmas holidays end on January 6. Figurines of baby Jesus are hidden in the *Rosca de los Reyes* (Bread of the Kings) a ring-shaped sweet bread. Whoever finds the doll must host a party with dancing and molé on February 2, *Día de Candelaria*.

In order to adapt itself to Mexican tastes, McDonald's introduced the "McMexicana" burger in 1999. The sandwich consists of a hamburger topped with guacamole (a sauce made from avocados) and white cheese.

FIVE MEALS A DAY
AND BEFORE-MEAL WHIMS

A Mexican saying, "*se me antojó*," describes a sudden, fanciful craving for a snack. The best known of all Mexican foods, *antojitos* are literally "little whims." Usually antojitos mean corn-based items, the tacos, chalupas, and enchiladas so familiar to Americans. In Mexico, these treats are sold by vendors or in small restaurants called *taquerías*.

Mexican food vendors set up stalls wherever a crowd will gather. Pushcarts become part of every festival or fiesta. Vendors may do business near the entrance of a public building or outside the church on a feast day. Back in colonial times, resourceful women supported their families by cooking enchiladas or quesadillas over a charcoal brazier on a street corner and

If you carve a pumpkin next Halloween, save the seeds to try this snack. Wash the seeds well, then spread them in one layer on a cookie sheet. Roast them in the oven at 375 degrees for 20 to 30 minutes to dry. Dot them with butter or margarine and return them to a 400-degree oven for 5 to 10 minutes, stirring frequently until toasted. Sprinkle with salt. Cool and eat. Store leftovers in a sealed jar for later.

Flan is a popular dish in Mexico, and by varying its ingredients it can be prepared as a main dish or a dessert. A slice of black cherry flan is shown here.

selling them to passersby. In modern times, street-corner cooks continue to do business.

Buying food from stalls first became popular during the Spanish colonial period. Ordinary Mexicans loved tamales and other traditional foods, but the upper classes scorned traditional food as the preference of commoners. They hired French or Chinese cooks and ate European dishes. For them, eating tamales was acceptable only in secret, at home alone.

During the 1800s, families invented special country picnics as an excuse to eat tamales. Clever *entrepreneurs* also decided travel provided a good excuse to indulge in favorite foods. They sold tamales from roadside stands and later in railroad stations. Parties where only tamales and hot chocolate or coffee were served were known as *tamaladas*.

Through geographic regions of Mexico, food varies according to available local products and cultural influences. Until 1910, most Americans knew only the dishes prepared close to home. When they traveled to fight in the Mexican Revolution, they were exposed to new foods they had never tried before.

A woman hands out free tacos for the political campaign of Francisco Labastida. Offering food is an effective way to entice people to come to meetings and events.

Antojitos can also be served as appetizers before *la comida*, the day's main meal. Some antojitos are less familiar to Americans than tacos or tamales, or they vary from our Americanized versions. A true Mexican taco is seldom crunchy and consists of meat, cheese, potatoes, or other food wrapped in a soft corn or flour tortilla. Americans eat enchiladas as a main course, but in Mexico, they are considered snacks. A Mexican quesadilla is a tortilla filled with cheese, mushrooms, pork, or squash blossoms, then grilled. Tostadas resemble those we know, fried corn tortillas topped with beans, lettuce, and other garnishes. Other antojitos strike Americans as less familiar: *sopes,* small corn cakes filled with bean paste, and *molotes,* fried corn pancakes stuffed with cheese and chilies.

In addition to antojitos, sidewalk vendors sell many other treats: *tortas,* popular Mexican sandwiches; peanuts coated with chile; acorns; cucumber chunks; hot roasted chestnuts; roasted yams; roasted ears of corn with mayonnaise, cheese, and powdered chile, or lime juice and powdered chile; beans; soda, **flan**, or rice pudding. They also sell fruit ices made of mangoes, coconut, or peaches mixed with sugar, packed in ice, and spun into slush. Hot or cold pumpkinseeds, shelled or unshelled, fried, toasted or salted, also rank among the favorites.

A woman sells homemade tacos from a market stall in a Mexican plaza. Mass-produced food is not as much a part of regular Mexican life as it is in America.

Traditionally, Mexicans eat five daily meals: a large one at midday and four light meals or snacks. Dinner, *la comida*, constitutes the day's important meal, traditionally enjoyed at home with family. The five standard courses begin with soup, followed by a "dry soup" (rice or macaroni), then meat or fish with vegetables and tortillas, beans, and finally a dessert of pudding or fruit, and coffee. In changing times, the bean course is frequently skipped.

Today's busy schedules, especially in large cities, no longer allow the luxury of a *siesta* or nap after dinner. Once, most individuals rested at home through the hottest part of the day and returned to work around 7 in the evening. Mealtimes have shifted to meet the demands of modern life.

Days once began with an early light breakfast of rolls and hot chocolate or coffee and fruit, followed by a more substantial brunch of eggs or meat. Today breakfast in Mexico might entail coffee, eggs, and corn flakes. Light fare in late afternoon, similar to what the English eat at teatime, curbs appetites between lunch and dinner. *Cena* or supper comes late by our standards, at 9 or 10 o'clock at night.

Just as food varies between regions of the United States—lobster rolls in New England to grits in the South—local products and cultural influences differ throughout Mexico. Rustic flavors are a trademark of Northern Mexico. Flour tortillas are more common in central Mexico. Cooking in the West Central is the least traditional, reflecting heavy outside

Before stores existed in Mexico, open-air markets provided a place to trade or sell goods. Today Mexican markets open once a week in rural villages and daily in cities. Vendors offer fresh food and colorful handicrafts.

People sit outside a McDonald's restaurant in downtown Mexico City. Although most Mexican families prefer homemade Mexican cuisine, fast food is becoming increasingly popular because of its low cost and quick service.

influences. In southern Mexico and the Yucatán peninsula, tropical fruits, vegetables, and seafood are popular. Oaxaca retains much of its Indian heritage when it comes to food.

Marketing studies show Mexican shoppers today prefer the convenience of purchasing frozen and ready-made foods in supermarkets. Modern chain stores offer international foods—sushi, pizza, and French bread. Most fresh foods—tortillas, meat, and produce—are purchased from food stalls, handcarts, or at outdoor markets. Market vendors sell meat, cheese, fruit, vegetables and ready-to-eat tamales, atole, tacos, sandwiches, fruit drinks, enchiladas, and soup.

A variety of restaurants and cafeterias operate in Mexico, and family celebrations today are sometimes held in restaurants. Mexico City offers international dining—German, Japanese, Italian, French, Chinese. Fast food has also arrived in the land of the Aztecs: the first McDonald's restaurant opened in October 1985. Now more than 175 restaurants throughout the country serve specialties such as McMexicana burgers topped with guacamole and white cheese. Other familiar chains such as Denny's, Burger King, and Subway are also located in Mexico City.

> Mexican outdoor markets are called *tianguis*, named for the canvas or plastic tarps spread on the ground and overhead.

Mexican cuisine has come a long way since the Aztecs, but their techniques for making tortillas and tamales have endured through the centuries. Despite the creation of new dishes through the influence of many cultures, one aspect remains the same. Today, as in ancient times, the food of Mexico represents a glorious celebration of life.

CHRONOLOGY

250 B.C–A.D 750	Tamales are invented.
1325	Tenochtitlán is built.
1519	Aztecs honor Spanish conquistadors with a banquet.
1521	Spanish conquer Mexico. Roman Catholic missionaries bring new ingredients, recipes, and cooking methods.
1530	Spanish bring domestic cattle to Mexico and establish ranches.
1680s	Spanish nuns create the Mexican national dish, *molé poblano de guajolote*.
1821	Mexico wins independence.
1863	French occupy Mexico. Breads and pastries become popular.
1867	French leave Mexico.
1859	First corn mill registered.
1890s	Electric corn mills operate.
1899	First tortilla machine patented.
1902	First tortilla factory opens.
1910	Mexican Revolution begins.
1917	Mexican government divides private estates into small farms.
1940s	Traditional dishes regain respectability as Mexican national cuisine.
1966	Frito-Lay begins to make tortilla chips.

1985 First McDonald's opens in Mexico.

1990 Tortillas marketed in United States.

1998 Mexican government enriches tortilla flour with vitamins and minerals.

2001 Mexican government requires that tortillas be made from only white corn.

2006 Public health experts express worry about the increasing popularity of imported ramen noodles, which are less nutritious than traditional Mexican meals.

2007 A sudden jump in the cost of corn tortillas leads to nationwide protests.

2008 President Felipe Calderón considers reducing taxes and trade barriers to halt the rising prices of basic food items.

FURTHER READING

Kennedy, Diana. *The Essential Cuisines of Mexico*. New York: Clarkston Potter, 2000.

Long-Solis, Janet, and Luis Alberto Vargas. *Food Culture in Mexico*. Westport, Conn.: Greenwood Press, 2005.

Martinez, Zarela. *Food from My Heart: Cuisines of Mexico Remembered and Reimagined*. New York: Macmillan, 1992.

Mayor, Guy. *Mexico: A Quick Guide to Customs and Etiquette*. New York: Kuperard, 2006.

Peterson, Joan. *Eat Smart in Mexico*. Corte Madera: Ginko Press, 2008.

Pilcher, Jeffrey M. *¡Que vivan los tamales! Food and the Making of Mexican Identity*. Albuquerque: University of New Mexico Press, 1998.

INTERNET RESOURCES

Lo Mexico

www.lomexicano.com
Cookbook author Jim Peyton discusses Mexican food and cooking. He includes recipes from Mexico.

Mexican Cuisine

www.mexico.udg.mx/cocina/ingles/ingles.html

From the University of Guadalajara, descriptions of the techniques, characteristics and ingredients that make Mexican cuisine unique.

Access Mexico Connect Magazine

www.mexconnect.com
This monthly online magazine features articles on the food, culture, customs, and celebrations of modern Mexico.

GLOSSARY

Ambassador	An authorized representative of a country who travels in friendship to another nation.
Buñuelos	Thin, sugar-coated pancakes or fritters popular at Christmas.
Chafing dish	A container used to keep food warm at the table.
Conquistadors	Spanish conquerors of the New World.
Crêpe	A small, very thin pancake.
Cuisine	Style of cooking.
Enchiladas	Tortillas wrapped around seasoned, shredded meat, cheese or beans, then baked or fried and dipped in or topped with spicy sauce.
Entrepreneur	A businessperson who launches new enterprises.
Fiesta	A Spanish party or celebration.
Flan	A custard baked with a caramel glaze.
Frontier	The unsettled region at the edge of a civilization.
Jícama	An edible, starchy root.
Lime	A caustic, white powder made of calcium hydroxide.
Marzipan	A candy made of crushed almonds, sugar, and egg whites that is shaped into various forms.
Molé	A thick sauce of ground chilies and seasonings for stewing meat.
Quesadillas	Tortillas folded over a filling, then grilled.
Smallpox	A contagious disease that causes high fevers and pus-filled sores that leave deep scars.
Staple	The chief commodity or food of a particular people or region.
Tamale	Cornmeal dough stuffed with spicy meat, wrapped in corn husks, and steamed.
Tortilla	A round, thin bread made of unleavened cornmeal or wheat flour.

INDEX

PICTURE CREDITS

CONTRIBUTORS

Roger E. Hernández is the most widely syndicated columnist writing on Hispanic issues in the United States. His weekly column, distributed by King Features, appears in some 40 newspapers across the country, including the *Washington Post, Los Angeles Daily News, Dallas Morning News, Arizona Republic, Rocky Mountain News* in Denver, *El Paso Times*, and *Hartford Courant*. He is also the author of *Cubans in America*, an illustrated history of the Cuban presence in what is now the United States, from the early colonists in 16th-century Florida to today's Castro-era exiles. The book was designed to accompany a PBS documentary of the same title.

Hernández's articles and essays have been published in the *New York Times, New Jersey Monthly, Reader's Digest*, and *Vista Magazine*; he is a frequent guest on television and radio political talk shows, and often travels the country to lecture on his topic of expertise. Currently, he is teaching journalism and English composition at the New Jersey Institute of Technology in Newark, where he holds the position of writer-in-residence. He is also a member of the adjunct faculty at Rutgers University.

Hernández left Cuba with his parents at the age of nine. After living in Spain for a year, the family settled in Union City, New Jersey, where Hernández grew up. He attended Rutgers University, where he earned a BA in Journalism in 1977; after graduation, he worked in television news before moving to print journalism in 1983. He lives with his wife and two children in Upper Montclair, New Jersey.

Jan McDaniel is a former newspaper reporter and the author of more than 20 novels. She and her husband live in Chattanooga, Tennessee.